DOMINICAN SPANISH

One Word at a Time

by Timothy P. Banse

DOMINICAN SPANISH
Dictionary Words and Phrases

by Timothy P. Banse

Learning Dominican Republic Spanish One Word at a Time

ISBN: 978-0934523-52-3

Cover, licensed shutterstock image.

**MIDDLE
COAST
PUBLISHING**

Good Books Are Where We Find Our Dreams

Slang is ever present throughout the world, in every language. And because vocabulary changes daily, learning the slang of a particular country, or region, can be a never ending task. So it goes in the Dominican Republic. Know that learning even a few words of Dominican slang can pay big dividends by way more enjoyable conversation, and even more importantly, to help you fit in a little better.

Dominican Spanish

The way the Dominicans talk.

Como hablamos Dominicanos.

Also known as:*Dominicanismos* or *Dominicanese.*

CONTENTS

A

A caco - to shave a head bald, especially when trying to hide hair loss.

A nivel - when something is pleasurable, or really cool

A po' ta' bien - Ah, it's OK.

Abombao - when someone had lots to eat.

Abombarse - rotten or spoiled food, fruit and water.

Abur-Abur - equal to bye-bye.

Ace - powdered soap, laundry soap.

Acechar - to watch or control.

Acetona - Nail polish remover.

Aficiao - to be enamored with, in love with or completely smothered by another person.

Agallú - greedy, one who does not share.

Aguajero - braggart, a bullshitter who talks a lot but does nothing.

Agolpear - (Golpear) to strike, hit.

Aguacero - a hard rain, a downpour.

Ahora - now.

Ahorita - Soon, later. In reality, perhaps never in Dominican time. Can mean both past and future depending on context.

Anchoas, anchoitas - pin curls.

Anjá - sort of like saying What! Wow!

Ajebrarse - to physically fight with another person.

Ají chili/hot pepper (Arawak).

Ajumao - drunk.

Al trisito - when something is about to happen or almost happened.

Alante - to move ahead, to go forward, to call the next person in a line. Similar to adelante

Alelao - As slow as a snail, a man who is a little slow or stupid.

Allantoso - Braggart, phony.

AMET - (El AMET) the traffic police.

Allante - liar.

Amemao - silly.

Amorcita - my little love (feminine or masculine), a term of endearment not necessarily love.

Anacaona - golden flower (Arawak).

Anda el Diablo - an exclamation with the emphasis on the word anda. Used like the word Damn! when surprised or frustrated. Translated loosely as The devil walks, or hanging out with the devil. (Often pronounced as one word: Andaeldiablo)

Añuga - to choke.

Apagón - an electrical blackout.

A su orden - You're welcome or, it's nothing.

Apechurrao, Apiñao, Apeñucao - to be very tightly, packed together like sardines.

Apiñar - to gather things or people.

Aplatanado - means you have become a Dominican because you have eaten your share of plantains.

Aplicar - to apply for a job.

Aposento - archaic Spanish for chamber, in modern day DR, it means habitación (room).

Apota - intentionally, deliberately.

Arma una piña - to look for a fight.

Arepa - the ubiquitous corn cake (Arawak).

Arrecho - for a man to be excited sexually, erect.

Arretao´- a very bold person to the point of being stupidly brave.

Aficiao - derived from the word asfixiado, meaning to asphyxiate. To be enamoured with or in love with, describes someone whose life/thoughts is/are obsessed with another person.

Asorao - surprised.

Averiguao - a person who is very nosey, from averiguador.

Avion - literally means airplane. A woman who does sexual favors gratis; an easy woman.

B

Baboso - an idiot. To speak lies, talks crap. Literally a drooler.

Bacano - one cool dude.

Bago - person who does not like to work.

Baisma - The basement.

Bajo - bad smell.

Bakebo - basketball.

Banca - place to place a bet, gamble (baseball, lottery).

Bandera Dominicana - literally the Dominican Flag. Also, the typical Dominican lunch of beans, rice, meat and a salad.

Bara - whip (Arawak).

Barajo - shuffled. Used when a plan was changed or did not happen.

Barbacoa - barbecue. A four-legged stand made of sticks, used by Taínos for roasting meat.

Basta - stop, that's enough. For further emphasis: basta ya is stronger.

Batata - sweet potato (Arawak).

Batea - metal wash tub, usually used for laundry.

Bayonesa - mayonnaise in Spanglish.

Beepear - pager, beeper.

Beibol - baseball.

Bengue - Ben Gay.

Bembe - big lips.

Bembú - person with big lips.

Bemberria - a small party for friends.

Bizcocho - Cake.

Bidón - an aluminum container, usually used to hold and

transport milk.

Bi Ma - Macdonald's ubiquitous Big Mac.

Bloque - Sidewalk.

Blumen - women's panties, bloomers.

Boca-aguá - someone who talks without thinking

Boca de suape -or Boca de trapo - literal means mop mouth, someone with a big mouth, a gossip. See Baboso

Boche - a corruption of the English bullshit, although in Dominican Spanish the word means a harangue. For example Me echaron un boche, meaning, threw me a boche, translates into they reprimanded me.

Bochinchoso - a gossip.

Bohío - typical small square countryside home

Bolsa - Careful with this word. In Spain it means bag, while in the Dominican Republic, it means scrotum. Use the word funda for bag.

¡Bomba! - Wow!

Bomba - gas station.

Bonche - party for a bunch of friends.

Bote llón de agua - large 5-gallon blue jugs of water that holds clean drinking water.

Bote - boat, freighter, a cruise boat.

Bozo - big moustache on an old person.

Brasier - bra.

Brecha - spy.

Brechador - man who likes to watch women, an ooogler. See Acechar - to watch.

Brechero - peeping Tom.

Brechar - someone that likes to brag a little.

Buquí - when someone makes a pig of themselves.

Bufeando - making fun of something or someone.

Bufeo - relax.

Bugarron - man who lays down with men.

Buquí - when someone makes a pig of themselves.

Burén - flat griddle.

Burriquero - out in the country a guy who rides around doing errands for people on his burro, as in trips to the colmado.

Burro/bruto - a dumb person.

C

Caballo - person similar to a tigre.
Cabron - a large male goat, also means displeased.
Cacaito - candy.
Cacata - tarantula-type spider, bad woman .
Cacharra - a vehicle in bad shape.
Cache-cache - means hide and seek in /French, in DR means cool, doing well. Also see Hevi.
Cachu - when you can do something fast, easy for you.
Caco - head.
Cacú - someone with a large head.
Cajeta - bag, can have many meanings depending on the context.
Callejones - a small road, alley. An unlit side road where delinquents, robbers and other shady people hang out.
Can - Celebration or party.
Cana - a palmetto palms.
Canillas - skinny legs.
Canoa - canoe.
Cansado - tired. Listen carefully so as not to confuse with casado - married.
Carajito - child.
Carajo - to say damn! or hell! without being entirely vulgar.
Carey - tortoise shell.
Carro - car (coche).
Carro Publicos - public taxis.
Ceiba - Silkcotton tree.
Cepillo - an old Volkswagen.

Chepa - used in the Cibao region for luck

Chamaquito - teens boys or little boy.

Champola - a drink of guanábana and milk.

Champú - Shampoo.

Chan - person, Man, friend, person.

Chancletas - flip flops, sandals.

Charlie/Chaili - person. See chan.

Chata - when a person has a flat behind. Also the small back pocket sized alcohol bottle that fits snugly in the back pocket

Chatica - flat bottles of rum that easily fit into a pocket.

Checkear - to check, investigate.

Chele - Centavo, penny.

Chepa - stroke of luck, que chepa! Que cheposo! - what luck.

Chercha - a joke, or in a party mode.

Cherchar - to talk in an animated way, derived from people gathering after church.

Chevere - Awesome, or cool. (African Roots).

Chichí - a baby boy. Usually a kid or a newborn baby.

Chichigua - kite.

Chicle - chicklet, the gum.

Chimicuí - can be a bad odor or a bad looking face.

Chin - a little bit of something.

China — this word pulls double duty. China can mean Chinese or Asian woman. But china is also the word for orange the fruit. In the Dominican Republic they only use that naranja for the color orange.

Chin Chin - a little bit such as in un chin más, a little bit more.

Chininin o Chililin - a very little bit, smaller than chin.

Chinchilín - from the Taino langauge, means a blackbird, to describe a really bad odor, malodorous.

Chivito harto de jobo - someone who thinks they're important but are not.

Chivo - goat, to be suspicious of something, to be doubtful of, to mistrust.

Chol - shorts, short pants.

Chopa - a denigrating word for a cleaning lady or domestic servant. It's rude to call someone this

Chopo - a person of the lowest class.

Chula - sugar mama, a term of endearment used frequently in the streets.

Chulea/Chulearse - to cover with kisses, to cuddle.

Chulo- a pimp, a player, cute or nice.

Cibao - Stoned Mountains.

Cicote - foot odor.

Cielito - literally little piece of heaven, used to describe a small tip given as a reward.

Cloo - club

Cloro - tu ta cloro estas cloro - the word cloro is used instead of the word claro (clear). So it would mean: I understand, you are coming across very clear.

Cloro - Clorox, bleach.

Cobrador - fare collector on a guagua.

Cocaleka - popcorn.

Cocotaso - a closed fist punch on top of the head.

Cocote - a person's neck.

Cocuyo or Cucuyo - firefly, lightning bug with a bluish light, known in legend as nimitas (the legend of nimitas)

Cohiba - tobacco/tobacco leaves.

Colín - the common machete. Derived from Collins & Company, a former Connecticut toolmaker.

Colmado - bodega, corner store in most neighborhoods. Sells drinks, food, necessities. Anything and everything.

Colmadón - a larger version of a Colmado. Usually has music, dancing, food. Closely resembles a local bar.

Compai / Copai - Compadre - friend.

Comparona - a show off.

Con flei - corn flakes, refers to any breakfast cereal, be it puffed corn, bran flakes, or puffed wheat.

Concho - (Con-Cho) - 1. A non curse form of the word damn (coño). 2. moto-concho - short way of saying public taxi

Concho - A public transportation vehicle

Coño - an expression close in meaning to Damn! (a little vulgar). Can also mean a woman's private parts (vulgar)

Cota - the dirt embedded in the creases of the skin around the neck.

Cote - Kotex.

Cotorra - parrot, a person who talks too much.

Cuarto - depends on the context. It can mean room as in rooms in a house or it can mean money as in No tengo cuarto. I have no money.

Cuco - the boogy monster.

Cuero - a female sanky panky. A woman who picks up tourists, claims love and uses them to finagle cash, gifts and other gains. Usually a resort worker.

Cuero - hooker.

Cuquear - to bother

Cura - a cure, something funny.

Cutafara - Ugly woman.

Cuté - nail polish.

D

Dale Pa'bajo - to chow down; when you have food in front of you someone might say this.

Dame Lu - a greeting What's up? or What's happenin'? literally give me light (enlighten me) Dazme luz.

Deguabine - someone in bad physical shape.

Deguabinar - to destroy.

Deja me — means leave me alone.

Deplayarse - laying around for hours doing nothing, maybe laying in bed and watching tv.

Detutanao - canceled.

¿Dime ave? - whats up? Tell me what's going on. Literally, enlighten me so that I can see.

Dímelo? - sort of like What's happenin', How are you?, typically used when answering the phone.

¡Diachi! - softens the word diablo (devil). Typically used instead of damn ie: Diache! You look good or Diache! That stings. Can express astonishment or surprise. From diatre, which means devilish.

Dios te Bendigas - God bless you! Your response is Amen.

Dimeave - abreviated form of Dime aver, tell me so I can see it. What's going on?

Dimelo/que lo que - what's up/hello.

Dí que - similar to saying uhhmm...in place of a pause in a sentence,from dizque.

Dry Clean - to clean up yourself especially before a party or after going to the beach.

E

Echar agua - to shower.

Echar polvo - to ejaculate.

Emparchao - stomach pain, indigestion.

Emperchado - someone that dresses in the high fashion of the time.

Encendio - having a good time.

Enchivao - clogged.

Enchivarse - to be stuck on a muddy road.

Enchulao - to be in love

Enchumbao - to be full of it, I am soaked, used to refer to wet shoes after a rain.

Enculillarse-to have a bad itch.

Enjaretar - to gorge on food.

Envenenarse - to drink alcoholic beverages and get drunk.

Eringarse - describes the Dominican way of borrowing money, spending it, and then borrowing more without paying back what's all ready owed..

Equivocado - literally means wrong, useful when disputing an issue, but best for explaining someone dialed a wrong number wrong number. Simply say equivocado and they will hang up without babbling on.

Escrines-screens.

Esprie-Sprite the soda.

F

Fajar - to fight someone or to get busy.

Fantamoso - a show off.

Fariseo - someone from another country who does not respect the locals, a bad foreigner.

Ferré/ Darce Ferré - to fix ones self up, to make up ones self.

Fiao - on credit, many Colmados and local vendors will take credit if they know and trust you.

Firbtu or Fiebre - Literally someone suffering the flu, or describing someone who is over-zealous about something.

Fifty - Fifty - a high class person.

Flow - good style.

Fó - expression used before a word for a bad scent.

Fotostática - photocopy.

Fria - cold beer.

Frio - cold, cool, chilling..

Fuego - used when you agree with something someone said.

Fui - Normally this word means I went but Dominicans use this for the word culo or butt.

Fulano, perensejo y sutanejo - used when you don't know a person's name (what's his name?)

Fuljean - full jeans, when a woman fills out her jeans nicely.

Fulillo /fuí - Anus.

Funda - bag, shopping bag. In mainstream Spanish the word is bolsa while in the DR it's a scrotum.

Fuñir/ Fuñe - to bother, annoy.

Freco - To get fresh (sexually or verbally), a smart mouth. Typically spelled fresco meaning fresh but usually pronounced without the S.

Fregada - bother, hassle, a nuisance.

Freta - when a woman's nipples are erect. Nipping out.

Frito — fried but commonly describes fried plantains, also called tostones.

Furufa - an ugly woman, not a compliment.

G

Galleta - a smack/slap.

Galleta — meaning depends on the context. It means cracker when talking about food as in galleta salada - a saltine cracker. But it can also mean a punch or slap as in me dio una galleta - he hit me.

Galillo - person with a loud voice.

Gallina - chicken, someone who's afraid.

Gato - cat, a robber.

Gase - burp, belch, gas.

Gillette - and its derivative yilé refer to any razor.

Glu-glu - like saying glug-glug in English; the sound one makes when drinking.

Gotea - to fall.

Grajo - armpit odor, underarm stink, body odor.

Grand mierda-- who cares?

Granja - farm/agricultural field..

Grexxxenye a - bad hair.

Grillo - woman of ill repute, uses you, then leaves you, usually has bad hair. Also a cricket.

Guachiman - watchman, private guard.

Guagua - privately owned mini-van used as transportation.

Guaifai - WiFi internet service.

Guapo - handsome or beautiful in other Latin American counties, but in the Dominican republic it means Angry, mad or tough, a tough guy.

Guaraguao - long, untrimmed fingernails that need clipping.

¡Güay ! - Wow!

¡Guay mi Mai! - to express pain

Guayo - grater

Gueje, gueje - ridicule.

Guineo - the word for banana in the Dominican Republic.

Güira - metal instrument, made of perforated metal, used as a percussion instrument in merengue and bachata.

H

Hablador - liar.

Habichuelas - beans, habichuelas con arroz is beans and rice. In the Dominican Republic frijoles is only used for fresh green beans frijoles verdes.

Hacerse el chivo loco - To play dumb and unaware. To be irresponsible, oblivious.

Hanguia - to hang out. Let's go hang out at the Colmado.

Hanguiadero - one who hangs.

Heavy - cool - Que heavy. (How cool) 'Ta heavy (That is cool)

Hijo de Machepa - a poor man who does not have anything but bad luck.

Horripilante - terrible.

Huidera/o - where a crowd runs to for action, where something is happening.

I

Impueto - accustomed to, used to, customary.

J

Jablador or Hablador - liar.

Jabladoraso - someone who exaggerates things or twist facts to get what he wants.

Jaiba - river crab or freshwater crayfish (Arawak.

Jalar - to put drugs up your nose.

Jamona - a woman who is older than 40-ish and not yet married.

Jaro - aluminum vase to drink water.

Jarto/a - very tired of something or someone.

Jeepeta - SUV.

Jevi - all good, all cool.

Jevi duti - looking good.

Jevón - girl, usually very beautiful.

Jicotea - turtle (Arawak).

Joder - to bother someone; to make love to.

Joe - when you don't know someone's name, call them Joe.

Jompear (yompear) - to jump start a car with jumper cables.

Jumo - a hangover.

K

¿K lo K? - (Que lo Que) - Whats up? Whats happenin'?

Kachu - ketchup

Kille -literally broken glass, to be angry.

Kimbo, po-pó, Jierro - pistol.

Kukika, carabelita - cheap, low quality item.

L

Lambón - someone who goes to someone's home and eats and drinks their food without invite, flatters someone for personal gain.

Lavagallos - literally rooster cleaner, bad rum used to clean the game cocks wounds, rot gut liquor or firewater.

Lechoza - papaya.

Likeo/Liqueo - a problem/something's up/something's not right.

Lon pley - long play, a record album.

Lio - problem.

Loco - Are you nuts! - ¡tu ta loco!/. Calling someone crazy.

Lonchera - from the English word, lunch, describes a child's lunch box.

Lo que va, biene - What goes around comes around.

Lua - a spirit protector.

Lunche - lunch.

Luz - electrical service, lights.

M

(la) Macaste - you did it wrong, or you messed up.

Machete - machete, a Spanish word, also referred to as a colín, derived from Collins & Co., the brand name of a former Connecticut toolmaker.

Machucar or Machacar - to smash or crush, as in I smashed toe.

Maco - literally a toad, though in sports it means someone who can't throw a ball.

Mai - mom, mamá, mother.

Maipiolo - a match-maker, looks for a partner for another, fixes someone up.

Mambo - style/swing, Lianna tiene mambo - she has style/swing.

MamaJuana - A typical Dominican drink made with herbs and roots with rum,honey and vine added. Sometimes animal parts are added, reputedly an aphrodisiac.

Mandamás - big shot, boss.

Manga ahi Manga ahi manin take that, that's what you get.

Manin - diminutive for man.

'Mano - short for hermano, brother. Used when greeting a good friend.

Manso, Mansito - tranquilo, cool, relaxing; chillin'. Can also mean a non-aggressive domesticated animal.

Mala pata - bad luck, the same as mala suerte

Maraca - gourd rattle, a musical instrument made of higuera gourd.

Mata - tree.

Matatan - big boss. Bossy, derived from monstro

Matantan - very street smart and hardcore individual.

Maricon - gay man.

Masamorra - athlete's foot ailment.

Mayimbe - boss, big shot, cool guy.

Me da grima - it scares me.

Me tienen en un tirijala - I'll see you soon or I'll soon be there.

Medio Pollo - coffee with milk.

Menta - mint, refers to all types of candy.

Meter - to eat something.

Mime - tiny insect, typically a fruit fly.

Mishu - how to call a cat.

Mistoline - cleaner.

Mol - shopping mall.

Mono - monkey, a person who is annoying

Moños, greñas, pajón, corbeja, afro - used to describe frizzy hair.

Montro - dude, buddy, pal.

Morena, moreno - brown skin. Someone calls out to another, Oy Morena!

Moto - motorcycle.

Motoconcho - motorcycle taxi..

Mueelu, Muelero - slick talker.

Muflé - a muffler.

Muñecas limé - a faceless clay doll in a long dress. The limé doll was created in 1981 by sculpture Mere Liliana and while the originalis no longer made, copies can be found in most gift shops around the country.

Mu, Muo - in a word, dumb.

N & Ñ

Ná - short for nada, nothing. Nada, nada, nada.

Nalgas - butt cheeks (in Spain, culo is used, which in DR Spanish is the anus.

Ñame - fool, idiot.

Nana or nena - little girl.

Ñañara (Saranana, guachipa, salpullio) - Itching, burning dermatitis.

Ñapa - a gift for buying a lot of things. Like the bank gives a gift for opening an account or you buy 3 and get 1 free.

Narana - the colour orange only and not the fruit.

Negocito - a small business. Usually meaning all the little vendors and shops set up along the streets

Nitido - describes something really nice, in mint condition

No hay problema - no problem.

Ñojo - said to describe something in very large amount ¡Que ñojo (gran) pescao! What a big fish!

Nueva Yol - Dominican Spanish for New York, can also means the entire U.S.

O

Ofrescame - surprised, oh my gosh.

Olla - signifies being in big monetary trouble.

Ordenar - to order.

Osten - someone who acts in a very arrogant way.

Oyé - said when someone wants to make sure they are heard, said 2 twice to make the appeal ¡Oyé! Oyé! listen up!

Oyéme - Listen to me.

P

pa' k - why, but why. Pa' k you do not talk to me?

pa´allá - over there. Where is the street? Pa' alla Accompanied with an underhand swish of the wrist.

Pa' po' la - when you take leftovers to-go from a restaurant to eat the next day.

Pai - dad, papá, father.

Pájaro - feminine homosexual.

Pajon - person with their hair all messed up wild and sticking out.

Palé - tripleta, the lottery, is combination first and second numbers of the lottery and pays 1000 to 1.

Palero - dates from the Trujillos era when one of his security forces was armed with heavy wooden bats.

Paletero - street vendor that sells cigarettes, candies and gum from a box that resembles a large suitcase, a pallet.

Paloma - love, a gentle person.

Palomo - one who deceives in love, a player.

Pampers - disposable diapers.

Pana, Panita - friend, partner, colleague. A friendly remark to greet a friend.

Panó or Panneau - those skinny horses that look like they are on their last leg, but in reality are very strong

Pana Fúl - a close friend.

Pantis - a woman's panties.

Paracaídas - someone who drops in to a party uninvited like a parachutist.

Parao - person in a good economic position. Also a sexual expression referring to an erect penis

Parejero - a vain person, to be vain.

Pariguayo - party watcher, someone who stands and watches.

Pariguayo - A fool, loser

Pasao - crazy. Used to disapprove of the actions of another person "tu 'ta pasao."

Pa' seguida - right away

Pasola - ciclomotor, a scooter.

Patana - big trailer truck.

Patatú - a person very upset, very irate.

Pavo - turkey.

Pecao - fish.

Pega cuernos - unfaithful.

Pegao - Someone who includes himself in an activity without being invited.

Pegar un di'co - to have a hit/popular song that everyone knows.

Pegote - a piece of something.

Peje, Pecao - fish.

Pelmaso - stupid, clumsy.

(te) Pelota - to hit, strike.

Penco - big, immense. Used mainly in the town of Jaragua.

Pendejo - idiot, person full of it.

Peo - flatulence, a stinky fart.

Perico Ripiao - the oldest type of merengue music made with with guira, tambora (drum) and accordion.

Pica-pollo - fried chicken. Can also refer to a restaurant serving fried chicken.

Picaro - person who never pays.

Picher - the attendant who receives and helps the passengers in a gua-gua.

Pico duro - smart alec, wise-ass.

Pilón - wooden mortar and pestle used for grinding coffee,

garlic and other spices.

Piltrafa - to be eaten by pigs, worthless, useless.

Pín-pún - the same, two or more things that are alike, or two or more people that look alike. Identical.

Pinta - in style, fancy clothes.

Pipá - packed, when someplace or thing is packed in tight with people, really crowded.

¡Pipo! - a typical expression in the Cibao area used to express surprise, Wow! Elongated pronunciation elllll pppiiipppooooo

Pique - to be of bad humor, in a rage, not in a good mood ¡Tengo un pique!

Plebo or playú - plywood.

Ploplo - soft, flexible muscles. Slang for when the rear end (butt) of a woman is loose and bouncy.

Pluma - water spigot.

Poli - cops, police.

Poloché - Polo Shirt.

Pone chivo - doubt, not trust.

Por la maceta - very good; excellent; great!

Porra - a person or place you don't want to be with or at.

Popof - a high class person (same as fifty-fifty).

Pote - a small sampling of something. ie. pack of ketchup or mayonnaise, a one serving bottle of rum.

(Tener) Prángana - to have a very bad economic problem.

Prieto - NegroPrieto - Black person. In the DR, people call each other the infamous N word and other derivatives.

Pariguayo - A fool, not considered an offense there unless preceded by an offensive word and depending on the scenario used.

Propina - tip, monetary gift.

Pulpería - to be overwhelmed.

Puta - slut,

Q

¿Qué lo Qué? - (same as ¿que pasa?) litearlly, what's happening? But means what's up? (also written as ¿k lo k?)

Que Lo What - how you greet friends and ask what's happening. Similar to : k lo k but half English.

Quebrao - man with an extremely large penis.

Quilla/o (se quilla) - to be upset, to bother something or someone; to be mad.

Quiniela - since most can't afford to bet, a group or community will pool money to bet on the lottery or sports.

Quinielero/ a - the person who takes the bets, many times having smaller winnings only on a few numbers (a la)

Guimbamba - to finish or end late

Quisqueya - land, in Taino. Nickname for the Dominican Republic.

R

Rapana - friends with benefits. Sex buddy.

Rapar - to have vigorous sex with a person.

Raquiña - itch.

Rata - it is the lowest form to call a person, worse than calling someone garbage.

Ratata/jevi/nitido/bacano/caché/bomba- when something is cool or of compelling interest.

Ratreria or Rastreria - scumbag.

Rebu rebolu a group of people fighting or disturbing the peace.

Rebulujado o rebuluteao - disorganized.

Recorte - a trim, as in trim the heir or the bushes.

Relambio - obnoxious.

Remenión - when dancing the merengue, the ability to rapidly move the mid-section of the body

Revejio - young person with the face or an old person.

Roca - rock or to be on point, to be hard.

Ron - rum.

Rufo - Roof.

(una) Rumba - a lot.

S

Sacaliñar - to throw something up in someone's face.

Sacando chipa - Being very angry.

Sacar chivo - to commit fraud (Trujillo is referred to as a chivo).

Samuro - non purebred, fighting rooster.

Sandmurai / chancleta sanmuria - flip flops.

Sanky Panky - Gigolo Dominican-style, derived from hanky panky. Its deeper meaning is someone who engages in sexual relationships with tourist in search of a visa, or gold digger who goes into a relationship with the intent of getting money or gifts from their partner.

Saranana - skin allergy.

Sabana or zabana savanna - flat grassland of tropical or subtropical regions

Segundito - when you ask someone to give you a few seconds more time. Give me a second.

(hacer un) Serrucho - to collect money owed to you.

Si Dios Quieres - If God wants.

Sica - poop, fecal matter.

Sicote - smelly feet.

Silebí - sealed beam, headlamp for an automobile.

Silin - Ceiling.

Silve - dysfunctional or inoperable, doesn't work.

Sin Verguenza - ill mannered, without shame.

Siro - syrup, as in maple syrup on pancakes.

Soba - caress.

Sobacco - armpit.

Soquín - odiferous, an all-around bad odor.

Suape - a mop or the act of mopping.

Suape - someone who is very drunk. Tengo un suape, I'm drunk.

Suena - literally to sound, or to get a lot of radio play, like a popular song or album.

Swiche - light switch

T

Tabacu or tabaco - tobacco (Arawak).

ta to - okay

ta pasao(= - he's or shes crazy.

Ta paso Tu ta pasao - to cross the line to overdo.

Tabaná - open handed smack on the face.

Tablaso - huge hunk of wood, to smack.

Tacaño - when someone is cheap, does not like to spend their money.

Ta´en olla - bankrupt, broke.

Ta' Pagao - when you have a connection with an important person in a high position.

Ta to - OK. If you agree with something said. Or, ¿Ta to?; Is everything OK?

Tató - bien good, fine shortened from está todo bien.

Teipi - scotch-tape, adhesive tape.

Ténis - tennis shoes.

Teshir - T-Shirt.

Te da una galleta or cocotaso - to slap someone.

Te e´plota - to strike or hit.

Tibiar - heating up water or soup on the stove. In mainstream Spanish the verb is entibiar.

Tichel, - borrowed from T-shirt, refers to a rugby shirt, association football jersey, or undershirt.

Tíguere - Not to be confused with tigre which means tiger. A Tígueres is a person who is streets mart, knows his/her way around.

Tigre - tiger, used to describe a person that is a go-getter, will do whatever it takes to get what he wants.

Tiguerito - little tiger.

Tinaco - large tank on the roofs of many buildings used to hold water for the times when the water runs out.

Tingola - throat punch, a blow to the Adams Apple (la nuez de adán) with the fingers

Tirar - to phone.

Tirijala - discussion.

Tiro, cartuchazo o plomazo - to shoot a gun or a firearm.

Tisica - sickly, skinny, or gaunt.

Tolete damn, or male genitalia.

Totao - someone out of date, out of style.

Tráfico - traffic police.

Tranquilo / Tranquila — means relaxed and is a common answer to the question: how are you? You can also combine it as deja me tranquilo to demand: leave me in peace.

Tripa - intestines.

Tripea - joke.

(que)Tripeo - What a pity. Que lástima.

Tumba polvo - A suck-up.

Tutumpote - person in a good financial and economical situation.

Tufo - bad odor, bad breath.

tu ta' - (tu esta) you are - ¿Como tu ta'? = how are you?; ¿Donde tu ta'? Where are you?

Tu ta cloro, Tu ta Clorox - You are Clorox bleach, to be in the clear.

U

Una Fria- A cold one, Una bien fria, a really cold one. This is how you ask for a beer.

V

Vacano - something cool. That's cool: ta vacano.
Vacuencia - poop, fecal material, used to tell someone they are talking nonsense (shit). This single word can cover an entire sentence. You are talking crap!
Vago - lazy.
Vagua - a small palm native to Hispaniola.
Vaguada - storm or torrential downpour.
Vaho - a foul odor.
Vaina - the Castilian meanings are sheath, pod, shell, shell casing, and hull (of a seed), descended from the Latin word vagina, which also meant sheath. While in modern day Dominican Republic vaina is versatile word. With a number of wide array of definitions, such as: A thing, or a matter, or simply stuff, as in give me that thing. Often used as an exclamation like Damn! (Que Vaina!) or can be used as if you were saying That's a shit. (es a vaina).
Vakan - to be wise, cool.
Vale - means a person from the campo/country person.
Veldá'? Son veldá - Is it true? (Es verdad?) Yes, it's true (Si, es verdad).
Verdugo - expert, executioner. Someone who is muscular or strong, someone heavy-handed

Vestida de Novia - another name for a beer. The coating of ice on the outside of the bottle.

Vidrio inglés - English glass, animal poop, when you're walking and you step on a pile of poop you stepped on an English glass.

Vientiocho - literally the number 28, means crazy, loco.

Viralata - used to describe a mixed-breed dog usually brown, and the way they root for food in the garbage.

Visco - cross eyed.

Vivaporu - Vicks VapoRub crema mentolada ointment.

Vividores - a hustler, people who live of the money of others.

Voladora - a small bus that follows a route.

Volteo - when a plate is filled with large portions of food

W

Wepones - weapons.
Wiki - whiskey.
Wiki-wiki - Clothing dye.
Woloroso - to smell good. In fact, holor miss-spelled.

Y

Ya — means a wide range of things from stop! When someone is bothering you, or that's enough when someone is pouring you a drink or offering more food, also when something is finished, or completed, like if someone asks if you have had dinner or if you need a taxi but already called one.
Yeyo - a person highly upset to the point of having a coronary.
Yilé - razor. Derived from Gillette, refers to any razor.
yipeta - jeep, SUV vehículo todoterreno.
Yola - small fishing boat. Many times used to smuggle Dominicans into USA.
Yunque - being in a fighting, roughneck mood. Also, a blacksmith's anvil.
Yuncazo - a type of punch that feels like you were hit with a bull.

Z

Zafacón - garbage can - bote de basura

Food and Food Words

Ahuyama - a yam used in soups to make the color
Ají - pepper
Aji Verde - green pepper
Albóndigas - meatballs
Alcachofas - artichokes
Algarrobo - nicknamed mierda en cajeta - shit in a little box, because when opened, it smells really bad.
Arbejas - peas
Arenque - stewed herring
Arepa - spicy baked pudding made of cornmeal and coconut
Arepitas de Maíz - fried corn meal cakes resembles corn bread

Bacalaítos - cod fish fritters
Bacalao - cod fish
Barbacoa - barbecue
Batata Frita - sweet potato fritters
Batata - sweet potato
Batida - a blender drink made of fruit, milk(Carnation milk or regular milk), ice, sugar
Berenjena - eggplant
Biscocho - cake
Bisteck - thinly sliced, beef steak
Bondelic - prune cake

Cajuilitos Sulimanes - a small, red, pear-shaped fruit, mild flavor, with a crunchy texture
Cajuil - cashew, the seed is the cashew nut, while the cajuil is the

orangish fruit that holds the seed.

Calabaza - West Indian pumpkin

Calamares - squid

Camarones - shrimp

Cangrejo - crab

Carnesion - Carnation milk

Carne molida - ground beef

Casabe - cassava

Cachú or Kachu - ketchup

Cerdo - pork

Cereza - The Barbados cherry is common cherry in DR. It has 3 seeds inside the fruit.

Champola - milk with guanábana

Chen Chen - pudding made with cornmeal

Chicharrone / Chicharones - Fried pork skins.

Chimichurri - hamburger Dominican style

China / Jugo de China - Orange/Orange juice

Chinola - passion fruit. Maracuya This fruit has a tart sweetness that is wonderful made into juice and ice cream. It is also grea fresh from the skin

Cho-Cho or Tayota - little squash

Chofan - Dominican twist to the Chinese dish chow fan, rice with bacon, chicken and/or fried pork skin. Egg, garlic, onions and other ingredients are also added depending on who's cooking.

Chuleta ahumada - Smoked pork chop

Chuleta al Carbon - grilled pork chop

Chuletas de Res - prime rib

Churrasco - charcoal-grilled meat

Ciruela- prune

Coco Tierno - coconut and milk sweetened to make puddling

Coliflor - cauliflower

Dominican Dictionary, Words and Phrases

Concón - crusty rice on the bottom of the pan
Cremor - cream of tartar
Crinchí - cream cheese

Empanizado - breaded (usually a breaded meat)
Entre Cote - boneless rib steak
Espaguetis - spaghetti
Espárragos - asparagus
Espinacas - spinach

Frio Frio - shaved ice with flavors, essentially a snow cone

Granada - pomegranate
Grei-frú or toronja - grapefruit
Guanábana - soursop, a tropical fruit replete with creamy white pulp and green spiny skin.
Guandules - looks and tastes like peas but a bit firmer
Guineo - banana
Guisada - anything stewed. Rés guisada- stewed beef; pollo guisado-stewed chicken

Habas - white beans/ fava beans
Habichuelas - beans with liquid and mild spice. A Dominican staple
Habichuelas con Dulce-Beans made in a sweet sauce closely resembles a pudding, a traditional Easter dish
Helados - ice cream
Hongos - mushrooms, champignones.

Jonikaike also Yaniqueque - Johnny Cake, fried batter with different fillings
Jugo de avena - drink make with oatmeal and milk

Kipes-quipes, Middle Eastern - fried street food adapted to the Dominican style. Made with bulgur (cracked wheat), ground beef. Can be purchased in Colmados in the morning.

La Bandera Dominicana - The Dominican Flag, typical Dominican lunch of beans, rice, meat and salad
Lambi - conch
Langosta - spiny lobster
Lechón Asado - roast suckling pig
Lechoza - papaya.
Limoncillos - also known as Genip, Genipa, Mamoncillo and Spanish lime, this fruit, looks like a lime but grows in bunches. Inside the fruit is cantaloupe-coloured and sweet
Locrio - typical Dominican home-style rice dish typically made with sausage, sometimes with shrimp or chicken.
Longanesa - Dominican homemade sausage

Mabi - natural juice
Maíz - corn
Majarete - sweet corn pudding
Mamajuana - A folkloric Dominican drink brewed with herbs and roots with rum,honey and vine added. May have animal parts added for men's potency
Mamey - orange
Mandarina - tangerine or mandarin, ripe January thru February and then again November thru December
Maní - peanut
Mangú - made with platanos, onion and oil mashed and typically served at breakfast
Marañon - cashew nuts
Mariscos - seafood

Medio pollo - coffee with milk

Miel - honey

Mofongo - made with fried green platanos/ plantains, traditionally mashed with chicharrones/fried pork skins. Served with a broth on the side for dipping

Molondrones - Okra

Mondongo - tripe stew

Morcilla - blood sausage

Morisoñando - orange juice blended with Carnation milk

Moro - typical Dominican dish of mixed rice and beans or corn

Moro de guandules - rice and peas

Pan de Auga - Water bread, eaten alone or made into a sandwich. Colmados sell them fresh every morning.

Pancito - roll

Panceki - hotcakes, pancakes

Panza - pig stomach

Pasteles en Hoja - a tamale stuffed with a variety of fillings

Pavo - turkey

Pecao - fish

Pechuga de Pollo - chicken breast

Pejibaye - heart of palm

Pepinillos - pickles

Pepino - cucumber

Pera - pear

Pescado - fish

Pessi - Pepsi Cola

Petits Pois - peas

Pica-Pica - sardines

Pica-pollo - breaded fried chicken

Pichirri - the tail of the chicken

Platanos de Caldero or Maduro - caramelized ripe platanos

Pollo Frito - fried chicken
Pulpo - squid

Queque - cake
Queso - cheese
Queso crema - cream cheese
Queso de Hoja - white, strong, round cheese, bocconcini or string cheese
Queso Frito or Queso de Freir- Dominican fried, white cheese
Quipes - bulgur roll usually with scraps of meat inside

Rábanos - radishes
Remolachas - beets
Repollo - cabbage
Revuelitos - scrambled eggs

Salpicón - meatloaf
Sancocho - signature dish of the country, a thick stew-type dish made with vegetables and different meats (beef, pork, chicken, goat)
Siro - hotcake syrup

Tamarindo - tamarind
Taro - spinach
Tayota Cho-Cho - little squash
Té de Jengibre - ginger tea, a traditional Christmas drink
Tipili - Bulgur salad, tabbouleh
El Tocino - bacon
Toronja - grapefruit
Tortilla de Huevos - Dominican-style Spanish omelet
Tostones - fried plantains

Uvas - grapes

Vainitas - green beans
Vegetales - vegetables
Verdura' (also 'verdurita') - fresh coriander

Víveres - vegetables, fruits

Yuca - cassave, a long tuber vegetable.
Yunyun (frio frio) - snow cone, shaved ice with flavored liquid

Zanahorias - carrots
Zapote - tangy yet sweet fruit, has a dull brown skin, sticky orange flesh, large black seeds and makes great juice an ugly fruit.

Axioms

Si Dios quiere — If God wants. Used when making plans or commitments.

A buen hambre no hay pan duro - When you are really hungry no bread is too hard to eat.

A caballo resaldo no se le mira el diente - Never look a gift horse in the mouth.

A falta de pan, casabe, dice el pueblo. - Make do with what is available.

Date brillo cadenita que tu mojo llega - Shine now for your day will come.

Es mejor andar solo que mal acompañado - Better to go alone than to keep bad company.

Lo que va, biene - What goes around comes around.

El que anda con perro a ladrar aprende - He who hangs out with a dog will learn how to bark.

El que quiere moños bonitos tiene que aguitar halones - If you want nice hair you have to pull it tight, If you want something, you need to work hard for it.

Nunca digas de esa agua no beberé - Never say from that water I will never drink. Don't say you will never do something because you may have to someday.

Si la vaca ha venden por libras, porque comprar la vaca entera?- If you can buy the cow by the pound why buy the entire cow? Refers to having a woman for the night or for eternity.

Somos un pai de come 'platano - when told the price of bread had gotten too expensive, President Hipolito Mejia said, "Man does not live on bread alone, eat platano and yuca."

DOMINICAN FIGURES OF SPEECH

A la brigandina - to do something fast.

A paso de tortuga - when someone is painfully slow. Walking with the speed of a turtle.

Abrir gas - To run away.

Acostarse con las gallinas - To go to bed the same time as the chickens.

Amarrando la chiva - literally roping the goat. To do nothing when supposed to be working, because roping a goat is too easy.

Amarrar los perros con longanizas - To be very naive and give away opportunities to the enemies

¡Ay, mi madre! - Oh, my mother An exclamation to mean oh man! or can also mean like Wow! sort of a surprised expressive remark

Caerle a la conga - Literally playing the drums. To jump on someone intending on beating him up. To beat him like a drum.

¿Cómo e'tamo'? - country way of saying ¿Cómo estamos? How are we today?

¿Como 'ta la cosa? - How's things?, How's it goin'?

Como tu ta? — Dominican slang for How are you? or Como tu estas? Dominicans tend to drop the s, so Esta becomes ta and gracias becomes gracia and so forth.

Conocer al cojo senta'o - Literally, to recognize the cripple, even when he's sitting down. To know someone's intentions when they haven't told anyone.

Cuando cuca bailaba - When people talk about the old times

Curarse en salud - To practice prevention even before there is a problem

Despues de la excusa, nadie se queda mal - After the excuses were made, everybody got along fine.

Donde puede — literally means where you can, used when traveling on local transport and want to be let off.

Esta bien - instead of esta bien, most Dominicans say, ta jevi, ta vacano, or ta nitido.

E' palante que vamo - We are going to go forward, election campaign slogan.

E' pa' fuera que va - Out it will go, another election campaign slogan.

El carro quedó debaratao' - when a car receives a violent blow
Entrar a comer ojos - Between a rock and a hard place

Eso lo sabe hasta la madre de los tomates - Everyone knows it,everyone knows even the mother of the tomatoes.

Estoy entregado en .... - like saying I am up to my eyeballs in ____ (fill in the blank).

Gallina vieja da buen caldo - to express that a mature women has more experience and that adds to their sex appeal.

Hacerse el chivo loco - To play dumb and unaware. To be irresponsible.

Ir por la sombrita - To walk in the shade of a tree.

La mama de Tarzan - describes something cool or someone good looking

La piña está agria - the pineapple is sour, when something is difficult (dura)

Llegó la lú - said when the electric service comes back on.

Lo agarraron asando batatas - He got caught with his pants down.

Má caliente que una vieja metía en fiesta - Hotter than an old woman in a party mood.

Me da grima. - it scares me

Me hizo plancha - when a person does not go to something that they committed to.

Me llevó el diablo - the devil took me, I am damned

Me tienen en un tirijala - when someone says I'll see you soon
or I'll soon be there.

Ni con Dios, ni con el Diablo - Neither with God nor the Devil

Ni fú ni fá - when something is congested or stuck, you can't
move forward or backward

Niágara en bicicleta - to overcome many problems, to go over
the waterfalls on a bicycle, a song by Juan Luis Guerra

No Dar Un Golpe - not to deliver an attack, or not to work

No hay problema. - Not a problem

No' vemo- Nos Vamos - I'm/we're going.

Un clavo saco otro clavo (literally meaning one nail raises
another nail). When you have a hangover and need another
drink

Pa' seguida - right away; immediately

Pajaro de cuenta. - People will call you this if you are not a very
trustworthy person. Tamaño pajaro
¡Por la maceta! - Very good; excellent; great!

Probando e que se guisa - By trying is how you will know

Dominican Dictionary, Words and Phrases

Que aperidá. - Used when something is amazing

¡Que Leche ! - If you win at the lottery or get a really good job you say this.

¿Que lo Que? - the same as ¿que pasa? What's up? What's happenin'?

E' Pa Fuera Que Van - And ahead/ forward we go. Leonel Fernendez campaign slogan

Saber más por viejo que por diablo - To say that old age gives wisdom

Sacar los pies - to move away,get away from a person

Se fue corriendo - he literally took off running, to run fast, go full throttle, fast

Se lo llevó quien lo trajo - sort of like you brought it upon yourself. When someone has a big problem the response is this, you made your bed now sleep in it

Si dios quiere - God willing. Not necessarily religious.

Si tomas Brugal tú resuelve o peleas. - If you drink Brugal (rum), you either fight or have sex.

Ta que echa chi'pas - literally throwing sparks, means being angry.

Te llamo pa' tras - I will call you back, In conventional Spanish-devolver la llamada

Te conozco bacalao, aunque vengas disfrasao - I know you even if you are in disguise, you can't hide your intentions from me

Te subi lo vidrio - shut the window. when you've had enough talking to someone or when you don't want to hear them you shut the window on them.

Tengo un arranque encima - to be in a bad economic situation

Tililí-tililí - repeating the same thing or story over and over

'Toy feo pa' la foto - (exact translation - I am ugly for the picture) things can't be worst for me

Tu eres muy jediondon y delicagao -You are very hard to please

Tu ta como un aji picante -You're mad as hell

Tu ta' pasao -you have really crossed the line now! more of a warning that a fight was about to break out.

Tu ta' muy quitao de bulla - What you call a person that is carefree

Vamo hacer un coro - Lets get together and hang out

Vamo pal pley - Let's go play. Refers to baseball the pley is actually what they call the baseball field.

Vamos a Ver, quisas ahorrita - when you don't want to do something but do not want to outright say, no.

Viene una vaguada - here comes a vaguada, or here comes a storm.

y e facil - isn't easy.

y e verdad - are you kidding me?

Yo estoy chivo con eso - I doubt it, to doubt something.

www.ingramcontent.com/pod-product-compliance
Lightning Source LLC
Chambersburg PA
CBHW060704030426
42337CB00017B/2762